Major C. B. Vyvyan

Precis Of Information Concerning The British Central Africa

Protectorate

With Notes on Adjoining Territories

Major C. B. Vyvyan

Precis Of Information Concerning The British Central Africa Protectorate
With Notes on Adjoining Territories

ISBN/EAN: 9783743683471

Printed in Europe, USA, Canada, Australia, Japan

Cover: Foto ©ninafisch / pixelio.de

More available books at **www.hansebooks.com**

PRECIS OF INFORMATION

CONCERNING THE

BRITISH CENTRAL AFRICA PROTECTORATE,

WITH

NOTES ON ADJOINING TERRITORIES.

COMPILED IN THE INTELLIGENCE DIVISION, WAR OFFICE,

BY

MAJOR C. B. VYVYAN,
2nd Bn. The Buffs (East Kent Regt.).

FEBRUARY 1899.

LONDON:
PRINTED FOR HER MAJESTY'S STATIONERY OFFICE,
BY HARRISON AND SONS, ST. MARTIN'S LANE,
PRINTERS IN ORDINARY TO HER MAJESTY.

And to be purchased, either directly or through any Bookseller, from
EYRE & SPOTTISWOODE, East Harding Street, Fleet Street, E.C.; or
JOHN MENZIES & Co., 12, Hanover Street, Edinburgh, and
90, West Nile Street, Glasgow; or
HODGES, FIGGIS, & Co., Limited, 104, Grafton Street, Dublin.

1899.
Price 3s. 6d.

PREFACE.

This précis has been compiled mainly from official sources and from Sir H. H. Johnston's work on British Central Africa. Much valuable information has also been derived from Major (local Lieutenant-Colonel) W. H. Manning, Indian Staff Corps, Commandant British Central Africa Military Forces, and Deputy Commissioner and Consul British Central Africa Protectorate.

GH,
D.M.I.

August 1899.

CONTENTS.

CHAPTER I.

GENERAL DESCRIPTION.

CHAPTER II.

CLIMATE AND HEALTH.

CHAPTER III.

INHABITANTS.

CHAPTER IV.

HISTORY.

CHAPTER V.

COMMUNICATIONS.

CHAPTER VI.

ADMINISTRATION.

CHAPTER VII.

ARMED FORCES.

INDUSTRIES.

CHAPTER IX.

APPENDICES.

MAPS.

CHAPTER I.

GENERAL DESCRIPTION.

Geography. Geology. Minerals. Natural History.

The territory comprised in the British Central Africa Protec- torate is a strip, about 520 miles in length, and 50 to 100 in width, lying, approximately, between latitude S. 9° 45′ and 17° 15′, and longitude E. 33° and 36°, and having an area of about 42,220 square miles.

This strip falls naturally into two divisions, the first consisting of the western shore of Lake Nyasa, with the high table lands separating it from the basin of the Loangwa river, and the second, of the region lying between the watershed of the Zambesi and Shiré on the west, and the lakes Chiuta and Chilwa and the River Ruo, an affluent of the Shiré, on the east, including the mountain systems of the Shiré, Highlands and Mlanjé, and a small portion, also mountainous, of the southeastern coast of Lake Nyasa.

The Protectorate has for boundaries, on the east and south the Portuguese sphere of influence,[*] on the west the British South Africa Company's territory, known as Northern Rhodesia, and on the north and north-east, German East Africa.

The northern and north-eastern shores of the lake are German territory, and a considerable portion of the south-eastern coast is in the Portuguese sphere.

The limits of the Protectorate were laid down in a Proclamation dated 14th May 1891, and the respective spheres of influence of Great Britain, Germany and Portugal were defined in an agreement with Germany in July 1890, and in a treaty with Portugal in June 1891.

The administrative area includes a concession at Chindé, leased from the Portuguese Government for trade and mail purposes. (*See* Appendix A.)

Mountains.

A very large proportion of the Protectorate is of a mountainous or hilly nature, which generally takes the form of lofty plateaux, rising more or less abruptly from the lower ground.

---

[*] A provisional demarcation of the Anglo-Portuguese boundary is now under the consideration of the two Governments concerned.

Lakes.

Lake Nyasa, the third largest lake in Africa, is a deep basin 360 miles long and 15 to 50 wide, lying at an altitude of 1,500 feet above the sea and closely approached, especially on the northern and eastern sides, by lofty mountains and tablelands which rise several thousand feet above it.

Its principal affluents, the Songwe, Rukuru, Bua and Lintipi are on the western coast, but are of no great size; it finds an

outlet at its southern extremity in the River Shiré, by which
its waters are carried to the Zambesi, and ultimately to the
Indian Ocean.

Islands are few and of small area. The best known are those Islands.
of the Likoma group, about midway up the lake, which derive
importance from being the head-quarters of the Universities'
Mission.

The level of the lake varies somewhat in proportion to the Level.
annual rainfall; in an exceptionally dry season it is said to fall
as much as 6 feet.

Navigation is everywhere practicable, but owing to the Navigation.
existence of sandbars most of the ports can only be entered by
vessels of light draught. During the dry season the lake is
liable to severe south-easterly gales, which cause a heavy sea.

The water is fresh and good to drink.   Water.

Lake Nyasa possesses few good harbours. The anchorages Harbours, &c.
of the various ports are, in most cases, much exposed to the
north or south winds, which sweep the lake from end to end,
and often cause a troublesome sea. The approaches are
hampered by sandbanks and bars formed at the river mouths.

Fort Johnston, the principal port, and the head-quarters of the
Protectorate's Naval Force is at the outlet of the lake. Other
ports are, on the west coast, Monkey Bay, Domira Bay, Kota
Kota, Bandawe, Nkata Bay, Florence Bay, Deep Bay and
Karonga. Of these, Kota Kota and Karonga are the most
important, the former being the trade port for Northern Rhodesia,
and the latter for the Stevenson route to Lake Tanganyika;
both are customs stations and stations of the Trans-continental
Telegraph Line.

The island of Likoma possesses a fair anchorage.

On the east coast are Langenburg and Amelia Bay, both
German settlements; Mtengula, where there is an excellent
harbour, in Portuguese territory, and Fort Maguire and
Makandanji in south Nyasa; the last named is important as
the possible terminus of the Shiré railway from Chiromo; it also
affords a sheltered anchorage for the lake steamers when they
are unable to cross the Shiré bar.

Lake Chilwa or Shirwa, south-east of Nyasa on the Portuguese Chilwa.
border, receives the drainage of the eastern slopes of the Shiré
Highlands and the northern slopes of Mlanjé. It is about
45 miles in length, and 50 to 20 in width, and has no known
outlet. The water is brackish.

Lake Chiuta, a few miles north of Chilwa, and also on the Chiuta.
Portuguese boundary, is about 30 miles long, and 2 to 8 miles
wide. The water is fresh, and it forms the source of the River
Lujenda which flows northward from it.

Lake Malombé through which the Shiré flows soon after Malombé.
issuing from Nyasa, had, some years ago, a considerable area,
but is now partially filled in by the formation of a reedy and
sandy island and is little more than a broad channel for the
river.

Rivers.

The only important river in the Protectorate is the Shiré, which issues from the south end of Lake Nyasa, and, passing through the reedy swamps of Lake Malombé, takes a southerly course as far as the Murchison Falls, 85 miles below the lake. Here it is deflected for a time by the western portion of the Shiré Highlands, which it skirts for the next 50 miles in a series of falls and rapids, rendering navigation impossible. Below the rapids it takes a south-easterly direction as far as its junction with the Ruo, 40 miles lower down, whence it once more flows southward for about 90 miles to its meeting with the Zambesi 110 miles from the sea. The total course of the Shiré is thus about 270 miles, the last 50 of which are in Portuguese territory.

Navigation on the Upper Shiré is dependent a good deal upon the rainfall for the year and the consequent depth of water in the river and on the bar at the mouth of the lake. Under ordinary conditions small steamers can proceed from the lake as far as Matopé, some 10 miles above the Murchison Falls.

The Lower Shiré is navigable as far as Katunga's at the foot of the rapids, 28 miles by road from Blantyre. In the dry season, however, the larger river steamers cannot, as a rule, proceed higher than Chiromo, 40 miles lower down.*

Between Katunga's and Matope no boats can pass.

Other rivers are as follows :—

The Ruo, the principal affluent of the Shiré; it rises in Mount Mlanjé and joins the Shiré at Chiromo. For about the last 80 miles of its course it forms the south-east boundary of the Protectorate. There are some fine falls at a point about 20 miles above Chiromo, where it is joined by the Zoa. The Ruo is navigable for canoes for about 12 miles above Chiromo.

The Lintipi, Bua, Rukuru, and Songwé, western feeders of Nyasa, take their rise in the mountain region west of the lake, each having a course of upwards of 100 miles. They all have a considerable volume of water in the wet season. None of them are navigable.

The Songwé forms a portion of the northern boundary of the Protectorate.

Geology.

Sir H. H. Johnston thus describes the Geology of British Central Africa.†

" The commonest formation, perhaps, is a mixture of metamorphic rocks, *grauwacke*, clay-slates, gneiss, and schists. This prevails over much of the country lying between the west of Lake Nyasa and the Luapula river, on the Nyasa Tanganyika Plateau, in parts of the Shiré Highlands, and north of the Zambesi. The valleys of the great and sluggish rivers, however, such as the Shiré, contain an upper stratum of alluvial

---

* For further information about the Shiré, *vide* pages 19 and 20 of " Information on the Navigation of the rivers Zambesi and Shiré," published by the Hydrographic Department of the Admiralty.
† British Central Africa, page 47.

deposit where the valleys are broad and the rocks do not strike through. The principal mountain ranges are mostly granite, and granite, with its upper layers often rotten, and even turned into red ferruginous clay, constitutes the formation of much of the Shiré Highlands. There is an outcrop of sandstone on the north-west and north-east coasts of Lake Nyasa, and to the west of the River Shiré, near the Portuguese frontier. Volcanic lavas and tuffs are present on parts of the upper plateau of Mlanjé, and at the north end of Lake Nyasa. There is a good deal of quartz in the mountains to the west of Lake Nyasa, especially to the south-west, and in parts of the Shiré Highlands (such as Mlanjé). The low flat hills in the Upper Shiré district are composed of marble which yields a very good building lime. Much the same lime is also obtained from places on the west coast of Lake Nyasa, where there must likewise be a kind of limestone amongst the low hills near the lake shore. The surface of much of the low-lying country on the banks of the Upper Shiré is little else than a deposit of the shells of molluscs, mixed with black vegetable earth.

The black "cotton" soil, which is extremely rich for cultivation, and is so much valued in India, is found plentifully in many stream valleys and depressions."

Minerals.

The mineral resources of the country have not as yet been thoroughly investigated.

Gold is reported by natives to exist both in alluvial deposits and in quartz, but its presence in any paying quantity remains to be proved.

Iron is abundant nearly everywhere; the ore is smelted and worked by the natives.

Coal is found in the sandstone formation of the west Shiré district, and round the northern half of Lake Nyasa.

Salt is obtained by the natives from the ashes of certain plants, and by evaporation of brackish waters.

Natural History.

Large game is fairly abundant in the Protectorate. With a Animals. view, however, to preserve it from indiscriminate slaughter two districts have been set aside as "game reserves" under the names of the Elephant Marsh Reserve and Lake Chilwa Reserve, and the principal game animals are scheduled under two heads, the first comprising elephant, rhinoceros, giraffe,* and gnu (or wildebeest), and the second : buffalo, zebra, pig, and the various species of antelope.

Yearly licenses to kill game, thus scheduled, are necessary, and are as follows :—

(a.) License to kill any animals in the above list in any part of the Protectorate—25l.

---

* The giraffe is not now found in the Protectorate.

(*b.*) The same, with the exception of elephant, giraffe, rhinoceros, and gnu—3*l.*

(*c.*) As in (*b*), except within the game preserves—1*l.*

Wild animals not protected by game laws include hippopotamus, lion, leopard, serval, cheetah, wild cat, jackal, hyæna, mongoose, and otter, as well as several species of apes and monkeys, and many rodents.

Birds. Among the large variety of birds the following are useful to the sportsman for food:—Geese, duck, teal, plover, woodcock, pigeon, rail, francolin, and guinea fowl.

Predatory species include eagles, vultures, buzzards, hawks, ravens, and crows. Herons and other waders are numerous.

Reptiles. Crocodiles are plentiful in the Shiré and the lakes. Land and water tortoises, lizards, and chameleons are represented by several species. Of poisonous snakes the cobra, mamba, puff-adder, and viper are found, but accidents from snake bite are not common; pythons, and about a dozen other non-venomous kinds also exist.

Fish. Lakes Nyasa and Chilwa and the Upper Shiré contain many fish which are excellent for eating. Fish of the barbel type are found in most of the streams.

Insects. The number of insects which, directly or indirectly, affect human beings is very large. Of the former, scorpions, large centipedes, a tick, called by the Portuguese " carapato," and the burrowing flea, or "jigger," are the greater pests, while wasps, mosquitoes, and sandflies are also troublesome. The "jigger" causes intense suffering if not detected in time, and a daily examination of the feet is recommended in all localities infested by it. The mosquito is not found in the higher districts.

Other insects which indirectly affect human beings are, the locust, which here, as elsewhere throughout Africa, causes immense damage to growing crops and vegetation; * the termite, or so-called white ant, which attacks houses, wood-work, and trees; and cockroaches and various kinds of ants which damage stores.

Tsetse. The Tsetse fly occurs in certain low-lying belts, especially where game is plentiful. Thus it is found in the Elephant Marsh and the Lower Shiré valley, also in a few localities on the west coast of Nyasa, in the vicinity of Lake Chilwa, and on a portion of the road between Blantyre and Mlanjé. The tsetse is not present at altitudes of 3,000 feet and upwards, and does not affect animals being transported by water. Horses and cattle can be safely taken through the flybelts at night.

Vegetation. The vegetation of British Central Africa is rich in a wide variety of species, since it comprises not only the tropical forest and jungle growth of the river valleys and lake shores, but also many trees and plants which require the more abundant rainfall and lower temperature of the mountain uplands. The highest levels are mostly bare of forest, but afford good pasture land, free from the insect pests of the plains.

---

* The locust does not, however, attack the coffee plant.

Much of the forest region has suffered severely from the wasteful method of cultivation followed by the native tribes, who were in the habit of burning large tracts in order to make clearings for their cornfields. Only one or two crops were taken off each such clearing, and the destructive process was then repeated elsewhere. Steps have now been taken by the Forest Department to stop further damage, and the cultivation and preservation of timber trees is carefully and systematically encouraged.

Among the important forest trees are the Mlanjé cedar, African teak, ebony and ironwood, all yielding good timber, and the Albizzia and other shade trees, of use in coffee plantations for tempering the heat of the sun. The following varieties of palm are met with: borassus, hyphæne, wild date, raphia and oil palm. Acacias are common everywhere. Several rubber-bearing vines are found among the forest creepers, and the sansevieria and aloe, both producing good fibre, are abundant. The papyrus is plentiful in the lakes.

CHAPTER II.

CLIMATE AND HEALTH.

Temperature. Rainfall. Winds. Health.

The climate of the Protectorate naturally varies considerably, according to elevation, both in temperature and rainfall.

Temperature. In the valley of the Shiré and on the south coast of Lake Nyasa the heat before the rains is very great, the thermometer registering sometimes temperatures as high as 118° Fahr. in the shade, though with a fall of from 25° to 35° at night.

In the height of the rainy season, though the range of the thermometer is not so high, the heat is often more unbearable, owing to the greater uniformity and moistness of the temperature. In January, February and March the thermometer may be 100° in the day time, and only fall to 85° or 90° at night.

But in the high-lying districts, which constitute the bulk of the territory, the temperature is at all times more tolerable, the average at Zomba, altitude 3,000 feet, being as follows :—

Dry season—May to September, 75° by day, 40° to 60° by night; September to November, 98° by day, and 65° by night.

Rainy season—November to April, 75° to 90° by day; 65° by night.

Rainfall. The rainy season corresponds with that of the high veld of South Africa, beginning generally about the end of November and ending in April, the heaviest fall being in January, February and March. In the valley of the Zambesi the lesser rains commence late in October and diminish or leave off altogether in December. The heavy rains usually begin about the middle of January and continue till the end of March.

The annual rainfall varies between 35 to 45 inches in the low lands, and 45 to 60 inches in the high districts.

In the mountains, however, it reaches, sometimes a far larger figure, as much as 106 inches having been recorded in 1895 on the Dunraven Estate, Mlanjé.

Winds. In the rainy season, the prevailing winds are north, and are soft and warm ; in the dry season a cold and dry wind from the south-east blows often with considerable strength, and with destructive results to crops and delicate plants.

Climate as affecting health. The climate of British Central Africa cannot be regarded, even in the higher districts, as quite healthy for Europeans, especially for those whose duties or occupations entail exposure to the malarial conditions which affect so large a portion of the country.

During the months April, May, June, immediately following the rains, these conditions are more prevalent, and that period is consequently the most unhealthy season of the year.

Malarial fever, with its complications, especially the form known as "blackwater fever," is the disease to which Europeans are most liable, and which often proves fatal. In "blackwater fever" one attack predisposes to another, and the continued residence in the country of Europeans susceptible to it is therefore inadvisable.

Apart from malarial fever, there is no prevalent disease of a severe type among either the foreign or native population, and in the case of Europeans, ordinary precautions with regard to exposure, diet and clothing are sufficient to preserve health.

At the same time no European whose constitution is not thoroughly sound should contemplate a prolonged residence in British Central Africa.

Flannel should be worn next the skin by day and night; Health if other clothes are worn during the day a change of flannel precautions. should be made before sunset, as there is a considerable drop in the temperature during the night.

The head and spine should be effectively protected.

In malarious regions mosquito curtains are a protection against fever during sleep, as well as against the attack of insects.

Moderation both in eating and drinking should be observed. Meat should be well cooked, and spirits avoided except at night. Drinking water should be filtered before used.

Natives of India suffer in common with other foreigners from malaria and dysentery, &c., but usually in less severe forms.

The indigenous inhabitants also feel the effect of exposure to malarial influences, and are, in addition, peculiarly subject to affections of the skin, doubtless often due to insanitary habits of living.

CHAPTER III.

INHABITANTS.

Population. Europeans. Indians. Natives. Native Tribes. Towns.

Europeans. The European population in 1898 numbered about 300, of whom all but about 30 were British subjects. This number has been practically stationary during the past few years, but will probably increase with the more settled condition of the country and the facilities for the development of trade and planting afforded by a better supply of labour and improvement in roads and other means of communication.

Indians. The Indians in the Protectorate now number about 300, exclusive of the troops; they are chiefly engaged as small traders and form a useful class in the community.

Natives. The native population was computed in 1897 at 688,000.*

Native tribes.† The native races dwelling in British Central Africa belong to a Bantu-Negro stock, with, in some cases, an intermixture of a former Bushman-Hottentot type.

This stock is subdivided by Sir H. H. Johnston into 10 groups, of which the following are represented in the Protectorate :—

1. Awa-Nkonde.—Embracing the tribes on the northern and north-western coasts of Lake Nyasa.

2. Anyanja.—A large and important group, of which the chief components are the Atonga, Achewa and Ahenga, inhabiting the south-western, southern and eastern coasts of Nyasa, the Shiré Highlands, Mlanjé, Chilwa, and the lower and western Shiré districts.

3. Alolo and Anguru.—Represented by a small section in the Mlanjé district.

4. Yao.—This group is not indigenous, but came originally from the coast, and settled during the present century among the Anyanja tribes in the Shiré Highlands, on the south-eastern coast of Nyasa, and at one or two places on the south-western shore of the lake.

Angoni. Makalolo. The Angoni in the south-east are relics of former Zulu invasions, and the name of the Makalolo on the Lower Shiré is derived from some Bechuanas of the Upper Zambesi who were

---

* Statistical Abstract, United Kingdom, &c., 1898.
† A full account of these tribes is given in Sir H. H. Johnston's "British Central Africa," page 389, *et seq.*

introduced by Livingstone, and became petty chiefs and head-men, and whose tribal designation was adopted by their followers.

On the north-west border of the Protectorate is found a **Awemba.** portion of the large Awemba group, also derived from the Bantu-Negro stock, who, though not living within the limits of the Protectorate, deserve mention as troublesome neighbours whose subjection will probably be necessary in order to secure the trade route between Nyasa and Tanganyika.

In colour the difference between the Yao and other races is **Colour.** very marked, the former being of a light, yellowish hue, and the latter, especially the Wankonde and Anyanja, very dark.

Both in physical and in mental qualities the Yao excel all **Physical and** other tribes. They are a well built, athletic race, good and **mental** brave soldiers, sturdy carriers, and showing the greatest **qualities.** capability for learning various trades and crafts. They are also good cultivators, and make useful servants.

Next to the Yao come the Atonga, who from the first have been friendly disposed to the white man; they are docile, and fairly intelligent, and are good soldiers, carriers and boatmen.

The Wankonde are chiefly devoted to pastoral pursuits, and are large cattle-owners, while the Angoni, though also keeping cattle, are more given to agriculture.

The Achikunda on the Lower Shiré are, like the Atonga, useful boatmen.

Carriers are obtained from the Yao, Atonga, Anguri, Angoni, and Alolo, the two first being the best. The average load is from 45 to 55 lbs., and the distance covered in a day, 20 miles.

The principal languages in use in British Central Africa and **Native** the adjoining districts are Swahili, Yao, and Chinyanja.* The **languages.** last mentioned is in almost universal use in the Protectorate, and is generally understood by most of the native tribes.

Towns.

Zomba, the administrative capital of the Protectorate, **Zomba.** occupies a healthy site on the east side of Mount Zomba, at an altitude of 3,000 feet. It contains the Government offices, official residences and head-quarters of the military forces.

There are also in it branch establishments of the African Lakes Company and Sharrer-Zambesi Company, and a few stores kept by Indian traders.

A good road connects Zomba with Blantyre 40 miles to the south; the journey, by Cape cart, is performed in about 5 hours. Other roads communicate with the Mlanjé district, and with Mpimbi and Liwondé on the Upper Shiré. Liwondé is the port of shipment of mails, &c., for Fort Johnston and the Lake stations.

There is a regular bi-weekly postal service with Blantyre, in addition to the north and south mail service, which is also

---

* *Vide* Books of Reference, page 53, *infra.*

bi-weekly, and also a station of the African Trans-Continental Telegraph Company.

The water supply of Zomba is abundant and good, and provisions are cheap.

Carriers can always be obtained in the vicinity.

Blantyre. Blantyre is the largest settlement in the Protectorate, and the principal trade centre. It is also the head-quarters of the Church of Scotland Mission, and owes its foundation to that society and much of its prosperity to the African Lakes Company, originally affiliated to the Mission, and still occupying its old station at Mandala, now a suburb of Blantyre. The town is well built, and, besides a large church and mission buildings, contains the stores and offices of the various trading companies, an hotel, post and telegraph offices, and private residences. There are also shops kept by the Indian traders, and a considerable native population employed as carriers, labourers, &c.

All the ordinary provisions and stores needed by travellers or settlers can be obtained in Blantyre at moderate cost.

The water supply is not good, being liable to contamination by natives, &c.

There are many coffee estates round about Blantyre, and good roads lead to Zomba, the Upper and Lower Shiré settlements, and to Mount Mlanjé.

Chiromo. Chiromo, the chief town of the Ruo district, on the Lower Shiré, is the principal port and Customs entry station in the Protectorate. It contains several trading offices and stores, and a club.

Fort Johnston Fort Johnston, originally at the outlet of Lake Nyasa, on the east side of the Shiré, has now been removed to a less unhealthy site lower down the river on the opposite bank; it is the head-quarters of the naval establishment of the Protectorate, and is a flourishing settlement with a station of the Universities' Mission and good stores.

Kota Kota. Kota Kota, the chief settlement in the Marimba district, is the port for Northern Rhodesia; it is a Customs station and one of the seats of the Universities' Mission and is increasing in importance. The cultivation of rice in the surrounding district is an industry which has lately been much developed.

Port Herald. Port Herald, on the western bank of the Lower Shiré, is the port and Customs station for that district. It possesses several European and Indian trading stores.

Karonga. Karonga, the most northerly settlement on the west coast of Nyasa, is the trading port for the road to Tanganyika. The African Lakes Company have a post here, and there is also a custom house and station of the African Trans-continental Telegraph Company.

CHAPTER IV.

HISTORY.

Part I.—*Before the establishment of the Protectorate.*

Very little is known of the history of the region now called British Central Africa before the middle of the present century. Jasper Bocarro, a Portuguese, is said to have been the first European to visit Nyasaland; he appears to have travelled, early in the 17th century, from the Zambesi to the junction of the Ruo and Shiré rivers, and thence *viâ* Lake Chilwa and the Lujenda river to the coast at Mikandini. 1618. Early explorers.

The enterprise of Jesuit missionaries on the Zambesi would probably have led them to explore the unknown districts north of that river, had not an order for their expulsion from all Portuguese territories been promulgated and carried into effect in the middle of the 18th century, an edict which doubtless caused a temporary cessation of the extension of Portuguese settlements in the country.

At the end of the 18th century, however, the Portuguese Government, alarmed at the possibilities opened out by the seizure of Cape Town by the English, authorized an expedition, under Dr. Lacerda, Governor of the Zambesi, which had for its object the connection of the Portuguese possessions on the East with those on the West Coast of Africa. The expedition proved abortive, owing to the death of Dr. Lacerda after reaching Lake Mweru, whence his followers, in place of proceeding to Angola, returned to Tete. 1795. Dr. Lacerda's expedition.

The real history of British Central Africa begins with the advent of Dr. Livingstone who, in 1859, after many years of travel and preparation, was placed at the head of a well-equipped Government expedition, with the object of completing his previous researches on the Zambesi. Livingstone had heard reports of the great lake from which the Shiré was said to flow, and determined to find it. After experiencing considerable difficulty in ascending the Shiré, he discovered Lakes Chilwa and Malombé, and on the 16th September 1859 reached the southern shore of Lake Nyasa, near the site where Fort Johnston* afterwards stood. The name of the lake was recorded as Nyasa by Livingstone, that being its Yao appellation, signifying "broad water," and synonymous with the word Nyanza used further north. 1859. Dr. Livingstone's expedition.

---

* The present settlement of that name now stands further down the Upper Shiré on the opposite bank. (*See* page 16.)

Livingstone and his party, among whom was Dr. (afterwards Sir) John Kirk, extended their exploration of the western coast of Nyasa to about half way up the lake, whence the expedition struck inland to the westward, eventually reaching Lake Tanganyika. While still engaged in exploring Nyasa and the Shiré Highlands Livingstone was joined by a mission, under **Universities' Mission.** Bishop Mackenzie, sent out by the two English Universities. This mission, under the name of the "Universities' Mission to Central Africa," settled in the eastern part of the Shiré Highlands, but withdrew in 1862 on account of constant conflicts with Yaos and the loss, through sickness, of many of its members. It was subsequently re-established in 1881 on Lake Nyasa, where its head-quarters still remain on Likoma Island.

1863. Livingstone's expedition was recalled by the British Government in 1863, chiefly owing to political difficulties with the **1866.** Portuguese, but its leader returned on his own account in 1866, landing at Mikandini in March of that year, and reaching the south-eastern gulf of Lake Nyasa on the 8th August. Walking round the southern end of the lake, Livingstone turned his steps north, but at Marenga's town, near the south-western extremity of Nyasa, his carriers, alarmed by rumours of Angoni-Zulu raids, deserted him and returned to Zanzibar, where they reported that he had been murdered by the Angoni.

Livingstone, however, pursued his way northwards, and an expedition which was sent out from England in 1867, under Lieutenant Young, reaching Nyasa by way of the Zambesi and Shiré, ascertained that he had started for the west in safety and unmolested. His subsequent explorations, up to the time of his death in 1873, were outside the region of the Protectorate, and need, therefore, no further allusion here.

1874. In 1874 the Livingstone Mission was founded, in honour of **Livingstone Free Church Mission.** the great explorer, by the Free Church of Scotland, and with a view of continuing his work in Nyasaland, the first party of its **1875.** missionaries was sent out in 1875, taking with them a small steamer, in sections, for use on the lake. They were joined in **1876.** 1876 by the pioneers of the Church of Scotland Mission, who **Church of Scotland Mission.** chose the site of the present town of Blantyre, and established themselves in the Shiré Highlands, while the Free Church applied itself to the evangelisation of the inhabitants of the shores of Lake Nyasa.

1878. In 1878, Captain Elton, Her Majesty's Consul at Mozambique, obtained permission to conduct an expedition to Lake Nyasa in order to report on the slave trade, and, by the aid of the mission steamer Ilala, was able to explore the north end of the lake, and to discover the Livingstone, or Ukinga, mountains on the north-eastern coast (now German territory).

The missions soon began to find the difficulty of conducting, in addition to the regular mission work, the trade operations, which were complicated by barter being the only form of purchase, and the transport service between Lake Nyasa and the coast; it was therefore decided, in Scotland, to form a small company for trade and transport, subsequently styled the "African Lakes Company," which was affiliated to the Mission of the Church of Scotland, and its head-quarters fixed at Mandala, near Blantyre.

This connection ceased in 1881, when, in consequence of certain abuses of authority by lay members of the Mission, which formed the subject of an official enquiry by Her Majesty's Vice-Consul at Quelimane, the mission passed under fresh management. **1881.**

In this year the Universities' Mission, which, since its withdrawal in 1862, had concentrated itself at Zanzibar, resumed work in Nyasaland, and eventually established itself on the island of Likoma about half-way up the lake, and 8 miles from the east coast, where it was less subject to molestation by hostile tribes.

Meanwhile the Livingstone Mission had been making steady progress on the west coast of the lake, and had, to a great extent, succeeded in stopping, by conciliatory measures, the raids of the Angoni tribes against the coast people. About 1880 the society resolved to remove its sphere of work to Lake Tanganyika, the relative position of which, with regard to Nyasa, was laid down in that year by the explorer, Joseph Thomson. A project for connecting the two lakes by a permanent road was entertained and financed by Mr. Stevenson, a director of the African Lakes Company, and the preliminary surveys were made, but the work was not completed.

In 1883, the increasing British settlement in Nyasaland induced Her Majesty's Government to appoint a consul, and Captain Foot, R.N., went, in that capacity to Blantyre, taking, as his private secretary, Mr. D. Rankin, who afterwards discovered the Chindé mouth of the Zambesi. **1883.**

During the past few years the Makalolo chiefs on the Shiré had much increased in power, two especially prominent men being Ramakukane, whose father, a Barotse headman, had accompanied Livingstone back to Nyasa, and Chipatula, one of Livingstone's old porters. These chiefs had been, on the whole, friendly, though at times showing a disposition to be arrogant and exacting in their demands. In 1884, Chipatula was shot in a quarrel by one Fenwick, an ex-lay member of the Scotch Mission, who, having been dismissed in consequence of the abuses referred to above, had turned hunter and trader on his own account. This incident led to the Makalolo chiefs becoming inimical to the white settlers. Fenwick was killed by the natives to avenge Chipatula's death, and the little steamer "Lady Nyasa" was sunk by them. A large sum was also demanded as compensation for the killing of the chief. Captain Foot, however, succeeded, with the help of Ramakukane, in restoring peace, and the "Lady Nyasa" was recovered. Still the demeanour of the Makalolos, as time went on, became increasingly insolent and hostile towards Europeans, both English and Portuguese, and constituted an element of danger to the settlements. **1884.**

Another and more serious danger arose from the conflict

with the Arab slave traders who had settled at the north end of Lake Nyasa. At the time of Livingstone's first visit he found the Arabs established in a few places on what is now the Portuguese shore of the lake, and at Kota Kota on the west side, where there was a settlement under the control of a person called " Jumbé," a coast Arab and a representative of the Sultan of Zanzibar, who claimed authority over the Arabs wandering in those regions. Arab caravans, trading with the tribes in and beyond the valley of the Loangwa, were in the habit of crossing the lake on their way to and from the sea coast. In course of time these Arab traders established themselves in strong stockades in the Senga country, through which the Loangwa flows, and then adopted an alternative caravan route overland at the head of the lake. This brought them into contact with the Wankonde, inhabiting a fertile district on the north-west shore of Nyasa, and eventually a Zanzibar Arab named Mlozi, who had commenced by trading in the country, proceeded to surround his trading stations with stockades, with a view to taking forcible possession of the district.

1884-86.

About the time of Mlozi's settlement in the Nkonde country, the African Lakes Company had obtained a footing at Karonga for the purpose of opening up communications with Lake

1887.

Tanganyika, and their agent, Mr. Monteith Fotheringham, in endeavouring to interpose between the Wankonde and Mlozi, was drawn into a conflict with the Arabs, who attacked and besieged Karonga. The Arab attack was eventually repulsed after desperate fighting, but Mr. Fotheringham, finding his position untenable, abandoned Karonga and, crossing the lake, remained at the north end until reinforcements arrived, when Mlozi's stockade at Mpata was attacked and partially destroyed. The success of this and subsequent hostilities early in the following year was, however, rendered incomplete, owing to the vacillation of the native allies of the British. A fresh attempt to break up

1888-89.

Mlozi's power was made in 1888 by a force of natives under Captain Lugard and other volunteers,* but, though a good deal of damage was done to the Arabs, it was found impossible to bring the war to a satisfactory conclusion without the aid of disciplined troops and efficient artillery, and after several months of intermittent fighting, Captain Lugard left Nyasaland in the spring of 1889. During this period, in November 1888, an envoy was sent by the Sultan of Zanzibar, at the instance of Sir C. Euan-Smith, Her Majesty's Consul-General, to endeavour to compel the Arabs to come to terms with the British, but the mission proved fruitless as the Arabs declined to recognize the Sultan's authority.

In the autumn of 1889, Mr. H. H. Johnston, Her Majesty's Consul at Mozambique, arrived in Nyasaland and on the 22nd October he concluded a treaty with Mlozi, who undertook to desist from further encroachments against the Wankonde, and peace was restored.

---

* Including Mr. Alfred Sharpe, now Her Majesty's Commissioner, British Central Africa.

The consequences of this war had, however, aroused a considerable amount of hostility against Europeans among the Yao Mahomedans on the east coast of Lake Nyasa, since it was well understood by them to be connected with the suppression of the slave trade. Makanjira, a Yao chief on the south-east coast, seized and illtreated Mr. Buchanan, the Acting Consul, and Mr. Johnson, a missionary who accompanied him in a visit made with the object of opening up friendly relations, and only released them after payment of a heavy ransom. This chief continued for many years to be a source of trouble to the settlers and missions, and was not finally conquered until 1895.

Part II.—*After the establishment of the Protectorate.*

The future of Nyasaland assumed an entirely new aspect on the discovery of a navigable entrance to the Zambesi by the Chindé mouth.* This opened up a direct waterway to the Shiré districts, and disposed of the obstacle to the development of the country, hitherto caused by its only means of approach being through Portuguese territory. Two other events, at this time also directed attention to Nyasaland, and the possibilities connected with it, one being the application for a Charter by the British South Africa Company, and the other, the despatch of an imposing expedition under Major Serpa Pinto, destined, according to the Portuguese Government, to proceed to the Upper Zambesi, and Lower Loangwa. 1889.

In the summer of 1889, Mr. (now Sir) H. H. Johnston, arrived at Mozambique to take up the duties of British Consul in Portuguese East Africa, and proceeded, as arranged previously to his departure from England, to travel in the interior with a view to reporting on the troubles with the Arabs. Mr. Johnston was conveyed from Mozambique in Her Majesty's ship "Stork," which crossed the Chindé bar without difficulty, and steamed up the river into the main stream where she anchored, and the journey was continued in smaller vessels up the Zambesi and Shiré.

Near Chiromo, Mr. Johnston came up with Major Serpa Pinto's expedition, consisting of a large native force, and an European staff, which had been deflected northwards after traversing the Lower Zambesi. Major Serpa Pinto informed Mr. Johnston that his mission was of a scientific nature, and that he was on his way to Lake Nyasa, and requested the British Consul's good offices to secure him from molestation by the Makalolo people, through whose district his route lay. In reply he was advised by Mr. Johnston that the passage of so large a force was in itself likely to provoke hostilities, and was further warned that any political action on his part, north of the Ruo would oblige Mr. Johnston to take steps to protect British interests.

* The navigability of the Chindé river was brought to notice in the spring of 1889 by Mr. D. Rankin, Private Secretary to Mr. Consul Johnston; the Portuguese, however, claim that this channel was described with the remainder of the mouths of the Zambesi, in 1861 by the late G. A. da Silva, an officer of the Portuguese Navy.— *Colonias Portuguezas.* Vasconcellos, 1897.

In his journey up the Shiré, Mr. Johnston interviewed Mlauri, a powerful Makalolo chief, who was equally hostile to the English and the Portuguese, and had interfered constantly with the river trade. The commanding position of his village at Mbewe enabled him to completely dominate the passage of steamers, which were frequently called upon to pay toll before being allowed to pass to Katunga's. Mlauri, in spite of strong advice to refrain from interfering with the white men, expressed his intention of attacking the Portuguese, which he subsequently did, and was severely defeated more than once.

Meanwhile, treaties having been concluded with the remaining Makalolo chiefs and with the Yaos round Blantyre, Mr. Johnston proceeded up the lake, leaving Mr. John Buchanan, Acting-Consul, in charge, with instructions as to the course to be pursued in the event of the Portuguese advance being continued north of the Ruo. After the first encounter between Major Serpa Pinto and Mlauri, Mr. Buchanan, acting on his instructions, proclaimed, on the 21st September 1889, a British Protectorate over the Shiré districts. Major Serpa Pinto thereupon returned to Mozambique for instructions, leaving the command of his expedition in the hands of Lieutenant Coutinho, who, after erecting a strong post at Chiromo, advanced up the Shiré to Katunga, 25 miles from Blantyre. An ultimatum from Great Britain to Portugal resulted in the recall of the expedition, which was withdrawn south of the Ruo.

Mr. Johnston, during his progress up the lake, induced the Jumbé of Kota Kota to place his country under British protection, and on arriving at Karonga, arranged similar treaties with Mlozi and other Arab and Wahenga chiefs, after which he proceeded to Lake Tanganyika. On his return an agreement was made with Maponda, a Yao chief at the south end of the lake, who had previously refused to treat, and by the end of January 1890, Mr. Johnston was back in Mozambique.

1890.

In the summer of that year an Anglo-German convention ratified the work of Mr. Johnston, Mr. Sharpe, and other pioneers of British Central Africa, and in the following spring a British Protectorate over the countries adjoining Nyasa was proclaimed. The Protectorate of Nyasaland, under the administration of an Imperial Commissioner, was confined to the regions adjoining the Shiré and Lake Nyasa, the remainder of the territory comprised in the British sphere of influence north of the Zambesi being placed, subject to certain conditions, under the British South Africa Company. Mr. Johnston was appointed as the first Commissioner and Consul-General on 1st February 1891 and, for nearly 5 years, also administered the British South Africa Company's sphere north of the Zambesi. The British South Africa Company, during this period, furnished an annual contribution to the expenses of the Protectorate, but in 1895 this arrangement ceased, and the company took the administration of its territory into its own hands. On the 22nd February 1893, the name of the Protectorate was changed to the British Central Africa Protectorate.

1891.

The new Commissioner and his staff arrived at Chiromo, in July .1891, in Her Majesty's Ship "Herald," one of two river gunboats recently placed on the Zambesi by the Imperial Government, and found that the British settlers who had commenced coffee planting in the Manjé mountains, had been attacked by Chikumbu, a Yao slave trader in that district. Captain Maguire, an Officer of the Indian Army, who had lately arrived in the Protectorate with a small force of Sikhs raised by him for police purposes, was despatched against Chikumbu, with the result that the latter was defeated and fled the country. In the autumn of the same year an expedition was conducted by the Commissioner and Captain Maguire against Makandanji and Mponda, slave-raiding Yaos, at the south end of Nyasa, which resulted in the former being attacked and his followers effectually dispersed, and the latter suing for peace after his town had been shelled. Zarafi, a powerful chief further to the east, hearing of these successes, sent envoys to treat for peace, and the district was thus temporarily quieted. During this expedition Fort Johnston was constructed near Mponda's village.

It was now decided to chastise Makanjira for his outrage on Mr. Buchanan and other attacks on the missions. The steamer "Domira,' belonging to the African Lakes Company, was hired and a 7-pounder gun mounted in the bows, by means of which Makanjira's town was bombarded, and after two days' fighting was completely destroyed, together with two or three daus. The town of one of Makanjira's headmen, Saidi Mwazungu, further south, was also captured and destroyed a few days later, in return for an act of treachery which had nearly cost Captain Maguire his life.

Kawinga, a Yao chief, living at the north-east extremity of the Zomba range, was the next to be attacked by Captain Maguire and Mr. Buchanan. After severe fighting, during which Captain Maguire was wounded, Kawinga sued for peace, which was arranged, and Captain Maguire then returned to Fort Johnston. Shortly afterwards, in attempting to destroy two daus belonging to Makanjira, on the 15th December 1891, Captain Maguire perished, and the "Domira," in which his party was conveyed, narrowly escaped capture.

This was followed by fresh troubles, in the neighbourhood of Fort Johnston, with Msamara, a chief on the west bank of the Shiré and Zarafi. The former was made prisoner, and afterwards committed suicide in Fort Johnston. Zarafi's villages in the plains were captured with the help of volunteer officers, the Sikhs, and a numerous Angoni contingent, but further operations were stopped by the defection of the native porters supplied by Mponda.

In February 1892 Zarafi again became troublesome, and his hill-town was attacked by Mr. King with the garrison of Fort Johnston and a large Angoni force, but the expedition met with a severe reverse, Mr. King and another European, Dr. Watson, being wounded, several Sikhs and Zanzibaris killed, and a 7-pr, gun and some rifles and ammunition left in the hands of the enemy.

1892. The next few months brought much trouble to the Protectorate. The slave-trading Yaos in the Shiré Highlands and Mlanjé district made constant raids against carriers; Makanjira crossed over to the Rifu peninsula and drove out Kazembe, a friendly chief, and then proceeded to attack Jumbé. There were, besides, internal difficulties between the settlers and the administration, over land claims. However, before the end of the year 1892 the Government of the country had begun to assume a definite shape.

In May, Mr. J. L. Nicoll took up the duties of collector for the South Nyasa district, which was gradually reduced to order.* Later on three gunboats, built in sections, the "Dove," "Pioneer" and "Adventure" arrived from England, having been sent out by the Admiralty for service on the Lake and Upper Shiré in connection with the suppression of the slave trade.

A German expedition, under Major von Wissmann, also came out with the same object on behalf of the German Anti-Slavery Society, and brought with it a steamer named the "Wissmann." Customs regulations were formulated, a head customs office was established at Chiromo, and steps were taken to institute a hut tax. The settlement of land claims was commenced, with certain reservations of Crown rights, and when all the claims had been dealt with, treaties were concluded with the native chiefs securing Crown control over the remainder of the land. Courts of justice were instituted, and magistrates appointed. The construction of a road from Katunga to Blantyre was also proceeding.

1893. In February 1893, a long-threatened outbreak of slave-traders on the Upper Shiré took place. Liwonde, the principal chief of the district, was concerned in the carrying off of some boys from Zomba, and a party who recovered them was attacked by his followers on the banks of the Shiré, and was only relieved from a critical position by the arrival of reinforcements. Liwonde's town was then burned, but he himself escaped capture for some years.

In March, a further reinforcement of 100 Sikhs came from India under Lieutenant (afterwards Lieut.-Colonel) Edwards, and later in the year 100 more were brought by Lieutenant (now Lieut.-Colonel) Manning. Police were also recruited from the Makua of Mozambique and the Atonga of West Nyasa.

During this year the Protectorate was divided into twelve administrative districts: certain administrative divisions were also defined in the adjoining territories of the British South Africa Company (*see* Appendix B.)

As a protection to the south-east boundary, Fort Lister was constructed in the Mlanjé district, and advantage was taken of the arrival of the Sikh troops to bring the neighbouring chiefs into submission.

---

* And in June Captain C. E. Johnson, 36th Sikhs, arrived in place of Captain Maguire, bringing with him a detachment of Sikhs.

The completion of the gunboats on Lake Nyasa now enabled a strong expedition to be undertaken against Chiwawa, one of Jumbé's headmen, who had been persuaded by Makanjira to revolt. After a preliminary bombardment his fortified town, about 5 miles inland from Kota Kota, was taken by assault, and its walls levelled.

Makanjira's settlements on both sides of the lake were next dealt with, and after the destruction of several of his towns Fort Maguire was built, on the south-east coast, to keep order in that district.

In the beginning of 1894 Makanjira attacked Fort Maguire and the surrounding villages with a large force, but was defeated by Captain Edwards with great loss. 1894.

This year saw the organization of the civil service of the Protectorate, which, with the postal service, was placed on a satisfactory footing.

The lake-gunboats also were taken over from the Admiralty, and the question of the contingent of Indian troops settled on a definite basis with the Government of India.

In the following year the British South Africa Company took over the control of their territory, and their contribution to the Protectorate ceased, the Imperial Government repaying the Company a proportion of the sum expended by them in its defence and development. 1895.

Early in the year Kawinga again became very troublesome, and, after an attack made by him on the village of a friendly chief, named Malemia, had been repulsed, it was decided to finally reduce him. His stronghold in Chikala mountain was captured by surprise and his power completely broken by a force under Captain Manning and Consul Sharpe.

Two other turbulent Yao chiefs, Matipwiri, and his brother, Kumtiramanja, were next subdued, and both subsequently captured.

The encouraging results of the new military organization shown by these expeditions enabled operations to be now taken against Zarafi, whose stronghold in Mangoche mountain was stormed successfully, and the 7-pr. taken from Mr. King recaptured. Zarafi himself fled into Portuguese territory. Mponda's submission was next secured, and Makanjira's new capital taken and destroyed, and his followers dispersed.

By this time matters at the north end of the lake had assumed a serious aspect. Mlozi and the Arabs were raiding in all directions for slaves, had threatened some of the Mission stations, and were openly defiant of British authority.

Accordingly, a force was organized under Mr. Johnston's personal direction, consisting of 100 Sikhs and 300 natives, and the following officers:—Major Edwards, Lieutenants Coape-Smith, Herries-Smith, and Alston, and several volunteers. The gunboats being insufficient for the transport of this number of troops to Karonga, the services of the German steamer, "Hermann von Wissmann," were fortunately secured, and the expedition reached Karonga at the end of November.

Mlozi's stockaded town was about 11 miles from Karonga on the south bank of the Rukuru, the passage of that river, about 6 miles from Karonga, being guarded by the stockades of Msalemu and Kota Kota.

In accordance with a plan previously agreed on, three divisions of the force, on the night of the 1st of December, following a circuitous route to the north, were placed during the darkness in positions commanding the approaches to Mlozi's town. On the morning of the 2nd a fourth division, with which were guns manned by a naval contingent under Commander Cullen, R.N.R., advanced from the lake, drove out the defenders of the Rukuru stockades, and reached Mlozi's at midday. The town was surrounded and shelled, and a sortie made during the ensuing night was repelled. An attempt at negotiation on the morning of the 3rd falling through, the bombardment was resumed, and in repelling a second sortie the Sikhs, following up a success, scaled the stockade, and the town was captured without serious loss, Lieutenant Herries-Smith being the only European wounded. Mlozi was discovered, after nightfall, hidden in his house. He was tried next day and hanged in the presence of the Wankonde chiefs. The remainder of the Arab stockades in the North Nyasa districts were subsequently destroyed. A new administration station was built at Karonga, and a strong fort called Fort Hill erected near the British South Africa Company's boundary as a protection against Awemba raids.

While this was going on in the north, Lieutenant Alston and Mr. A. J. Swann had been making an expedition in the Marimba country against Saidi Mwazungu and Mwasi. The former surrendered, and the capital of the latter was stormed and taken. Mwasi escaped capture, but soon afterwards committed suicide.

The campaign closed with the driving out of two Yao robber chiefs, Tambala and Mpemba, who had settled in the Central Angoniland district. Tambala's stronghold was captured, and he himself fled. Mpemba was afterwards taken prisoner.

To guard the approaches to the Protectorate from the eastward a strong fort was built during the summer of 1895 on the site of Zarafi's town on Mangoche mountain.

1896. In the autumn of 1896 raids were made by the southern Angoni into the south-western portion of the Protectorate, and were punished by a force despatched against the chiefs Chikusi and Odete under Captains Stewart and Manning and Lieutenant Alston.

1897. Punitive expeditions were necessitated in August 1897 against the Anguru of Lake Chilwa for highway robbery on the Protectorate roads, and against Mpezeni, chief of the Angoni Zulus, in December; the latter had threatened the safety of the European settlers at Loangweni, and a force of 800 Protectorate troops, under Lieut.-Colonel Manning and Captain Brake, with guns and Maxims, was despatched against him.

Loangweni was relieved, and the Angoni Zulus punished. A fort was erected on the boundary of the Protectorate, and named Fort Jameson. This expedition did not return until May 1898 ; it suffered greatly from malarial fever.

With the cessation of raids, and the confidence now reposed in the Administration by the natives, the country is fast assuming an improved aspect. Roads are being constructed in all directions, and experimental planting is being carried out at various points to test the productive capabilities of the Protectorate. A regular armed force and strongly fortified posts guard the boundaries from inroads; the lake is patrolled by gunboats, mail and telegraph services are in working order, and if, as is hoped, the increase of cultivation and the consequent decrease of waste land and jungle, tend to improve the health conditions for European settlers, there seems every reason to look for a rapidly growing prosperity.

1898.

CHAPTER V.

COMMUNICATIONS.

Waterways. Roads. Railways. Postal and Telegraph Services.

Waterways With the exception of 50 miles of the Shiré River, between Katunga's and Matopé, there is good water communication throughout the whole length of the Protectorate, and between it and the seaport of Chindé.

Chindé river. As there is, at springtides, as much as 20 feet of water on the Chindé bar, vessels of considerable tonnage can safely enter the river and find a good and sheltered anchorage off the British Concession.

Zambesi and Lower Shiré. Traffic above Chindé on the Zambesi and Lower Shiré is carried out by several specially constructed light-draught steamers and numerous lighters, boats, and native craft, which convey passengers and cargo to the Lower Shiré settlements of Port Herald, Chiromo, and Katunga's.

Navigation. The navigation of these waters under ordinary circumstances presents no difficulty since the snags and other obstructions in the Lower Shiré were removed. In the dry season, however, the lowness of the river renders Katunga's accessible to small steamers only, and makes navigation slower in the lower waters.

Steamers. In 1898 the steamers trading on the Zambesi and Lower Shiré were 10 in number, owned as follows :—

African Lakes Company	4
Sharrer Zambesi Trading Company ..	2
International Flotilla Company	3
Deuss, Vertin & Co.	1
Total	10

Duration of journey. The time occupied in the journey between Chindé and the Lower Shiré ports is as under :—

	Days.	
	Dry season.	Wet season.
Chindé to Port Herald..	5 to 6	3½ to 4
„ Chiromo	6 to 7	4 to 4½
„ Katunga's	8 to 10	5 to 5½

Upper Shiré. Navigation on the Upper Shiré is confined to vessels of very light draught, owing to the existence of a bar at the outlet of

Lake Nyasa, 3½ miles above Fort Johnston, and to the shallowness of the river. Small steamers can get as far as Matopé, where cargo, coming overland from Katunga's, is usually shipped, but the mail route is by Liwondé, nearer the lake. A short distance below Liwondé there is a rapid, difficult to traverse when the river is low. The Administration steamers can cross the bar during the rainy season, *i.e.*, practically, from January to May, and, should the lake keep up, sometimes for some months later. The depth of water on the bar is from 7 to 10 feet in the rainy season, and usually less than 5 feet in the dry season.

At Liwondé there is a Government ferry over the river in Ferry. connection with the carrier road to Umlanjeni, &c.

The following companies have steamers on the Upper Shiré Steamers. (in addition to the Protectorate steamer "Dove," which runs between Liwondé and Fort Johnston).

African Lakes Company	2
Sharrer Zambesi Trading Company ..	1
International Flotilla Company ·· ..	1
Total	4

The journey from Matopé to Liwondé by water takes 8 hours, and that from Liwondé to Fort Johnston 12 hours.

Regular monthly communication with the various adminis- Lake Nyasa. tration stations on the coasts of Lake Nyasa is maintained by Steamers. the Protectorate vessels "Adventure" and "Pioneer." Besides these there are four steamers, owned thus—

African Lakes Company	2
African Trans-Continental Telegraph Company	1
German Government	1
	4

The last-named carries general cargo as well as mails, &c., for the German Protectorate.

The time occupied in actual steaming to the different ports Time table. is as follows. Average speed 6 miles an hour :—

					Hours.
Fort Johnston to Monkey Bay		..	..		4
„	„ Kota Kota ..	..	..		16
„	„ Nkata Bay ..	..	..		28
„	„ Deep Bay ..	..	..		35
„	„ Karonga ..	..	..		41
Monkey Bay	„ Fort Maguire	..	..		4

Langenburg (German Settlement) is 5 hours' steam from Karonga.

Roads.

Driving roads. The road communication generally is good, and is being rapidly extended. At present there are two good roads, available for wheeled transport, in the Shiré Highlands.

Katunga's— Blantyre— Matopé. 1. Katunga's—Blantyre—Matopé, 55 miles.
This is the main trade and transport route between the Lower and Upper Shiré, and is sufficiently good to admit of a traction engine working over a considerable portion of its length. The last 12 miles of this road, from the Larangwé river to Matopé, is infested by the Tsetse fly.

Blantyre— Zomba. 2. Blantyre—Zomba, 40 miles.
This road branches off from the Blantyre—Matopé road a few miles outside the former place. It is in excellent order, and admits of the distance between the two terminal points being covered in 5 hours by a Cape cart drawn by horses or mules. This road is in process of extension to Liwondé, 30 miles beyond Zomba.

Wagon road, Domira Bay. A good wagon road has been constructed by the Dutch Mission from Domira Bay, in Central Angoniland, to their settlement at Mvera, 25 miles inland.

Carrier roads. All other roads may be classed as carrier roads; they consist of a track cleared, to a certain width, of grass and scrub, and require periodical attention to prevent their being overgrown.

In the Shiré Highlands there are good carrier roads in all directions, and the system is being further extended.

Roads lead to Mlanjé from Zomba, Blantyre and Chiromo. Chiromo is connected by other roads with Chikwawa, Cholo and Blantyre, and from Zomba there is carrier communication with Mpimbi and Liwondé.

Other main carrier roads in the Protectorate are—

1. Liwondé to Mpseni's and thence to the Loangwa and Northern Rhodesia. This is a new route, and one which leads more directly to Northern Rhodesia than the alternative road from Kota Kota, and obviates the delays entailed by the lake journey to the latter point. This road passes by Umlanjeni's (Kirk mountains), the Angoni plateau, Mount Dedza—Chirenje, and Fort Manning (sources of the Bua river). A Government ferry at Liwondé connects with the roads from Zomba, &c. The journey to Mpseni's takes about 10 days.

2. Kota Kota to Mpseni's, by way of Fort Alston (Mwasi's) and Fort Jameson; the trade route hitherto generally used between Nyasa and the Loangwa valley. Time occupied by journey about 6 days.

3. Chikusis to Mount Dedza, a road from the extreme southwest of Nyasa to the Kirk mountains. Time, 1 day.

4. The Stevenson road, Karonga to Tanganyika. The trade route for the northern part of the Protectorate leading on to the Nyasa Tanganyika plateau. This journey takes about 10 days.

Where the roads are hard enough, and the Tsetse fly does Transport. not molest transport animals, wagons and carts, drawn by oxen, Draught horses or mules, are used. animals.

A traction engine, owned by the African Lakes Company, Traction works on the Katunga's—Blantyre—Matopé road. engine.

In other cases native porters are employed, the load being Porters. from 45 lb. to 55 lb. per carrier. Porters can be obtained at most of the administration stations.

The "machilla," a hammock slung on a pole, is universally Machilla. employed by European travellers.

The distance covered by carriers or porters is about 20 Rate of miles a day without relays. travelling.

Bicycles can be used on many of the roads mentioned Bicycles. above, but the country is hilly as a rule. Tyres adapted for tropical climates are necessary.

Railways.

The survey of a proposed line of railway from Chiromo to Railways. the navigable waters of the Upper Shiré has been completed. An extension of the survey, via Zomba to Makandanjis, at the south-eastern extremity of Lake Nyasa has also been carried out.

Postal Service.

The postal service includes the reception and despatch of Postal service. ocean mails at Chindé, where a postal establishment, under the direction of a Vice-Consul and Agent, is maintained on the British Concession by the Administration.

Ocean mails arrive and depart fortnightly in steamers belong- Ocean mails. ing to Messrs. Rennie & Sons, trading between Durban and Quelimane, and to the Deutsche-Ost-Afrika-Linie, between Beira and Mozambique. Both lines call at intermediate ports.

Mails are made up at Chindé for the Protectorate, North Protectorate Rhodesia, and the German and Portuguese territories on the mails. the Zambesi, Shiré and Nyasa.

Protectorate mails are conveyed by water to Chiromo and thence by relays of carriers to the post offices at Blantyre, Zomba and Mlanjé. From these stations the distribution is completed by a further carrier system, the mails for the lake stations being forwarded by water from Liwondé. The carriers travel in pairs and are armed with rifles as a protection against lions and other dangers of the road.

Post offices are in existence at all Administration stations Post offices. throughout the Protectorate. There is also an office at Cholo,

Time table.   The following table shows the time occupied in the transit of mails between Chiromo and Fort Johnston in the latter half of 1898:—

TRUNK MAIL SERVICE.

North Mail.

Bi-Weekly Service.

	Arrival.	Departure.	Letter box closes.
Chiromo ..	.. ..	Monday, 8 a.m. ..	7 a.m.
Cholo ..	.. ..	„ 8 p.m. ..	5 p.m.
Blantyre ..	Tuesday, 6 a.m. ..	Tuesday, 6 a.m. ..	Monday, 4.30 p.m.
Namazi ..	.. ..	„ 12 a.m. ..	
Zomba.. ..	Tuesday, 6 p.m. ..	„ 6 p.m. ..	Tuesday, 3.80 p.m.
Likwenu ..	.. ..	„ 11 p.m. ..	
Liwoudé ..	Wednesday, 5 a.m.	Wednesday, 5 a.m.	„ 5 p.m.
Fort Johnston	„ 6 p.m.	.. ..	

Chiromo ..	.. ..	Thursday, 8 a.m. ..	7 a.m.
Cholo	.. ..	„ 8 p.m. ..	5 p.m.
Blantyre ..	Friday, 6 a.m. ..	Friday, 5 p.m. ..	4.30 p.m.
Namazi ..	.. ..	Saturday, 1 a.m. ..	
Zomba.. ..	Saturday, 8 a.m. ..	.. ..	

South Mail.

Bi-Weekly Service.

Fort Johnston ..	.. ..	Friday, 6 a.m. ..	Thursday, 4.30 p.m.
Liwondé ..	.. ..	„ 6 p.m. ..	Friday, 4 p.m.
Likwenu ..	.. ..	„ 11 p.m. ..	
Zomba.. ..	Saturday, 6 a.m. ..	Saturday, 6 a.m. ..	„ 3 p.m.
Namazi ..	„ 12 p.m. ..	„ 12 a.m. ..	

Blantyre ..	.. ..	Saturday, 6 p.m. ..	10.30 a.m.
Cholo	Sunday, 6 p.m. ..	Sunday, 3 a.m. ..	Saturday, 12 a.m.
Chiromo ..	Sunday, 6 p.m. ..	.. ..	

Zomba.. ..	.. ..	Monday, 5 p.m. ..	3 p.m.
Namasi ..	.. ..	„ 11 p.m. ..	
Blantyre ..	Tuesday, 7 a.m. ..	Tuesday, 5 p.m. ..	3.30 p.m.
Cholo	Wednesday, 3 a.m.	Wednesday, 3 a.m.	Tuesday, 5 p.m.
Chiromo ..	Wednesday, 6 p.m.	.. ..	

Blantyre and Zomba Mail Service.

In addition to the bi-weekly service in either direction included in the Trunk mail service, there will be a separate service as follows:—

	Arrival.	Departure.	Letter box closes.
Zomba..	.. ..	Tuesday, 5 p.m. ..	3.30 p.m.
Blantyre	.. Wednesday, 7 a.m.	.. ..	
Zomba..	.. ..	Thursday, 5 p.m...	3.30 p.m.
Blantyre	.. Friday 7 a.m. ..	.. ..	

	Arrival.	Departure.	Letter box closes.
Blantyre	.. .. ..	Wednesday, 5 p.m.	4.30 p.m.
Zomba..	.. Thursday, 7 a.m...	.. ..	
Blantyre	.. .. ..	Sunday, 6 p.m. ..	Saturday, 11 a.m.
Zomba..	.. Monday, 7 a.m. ..	.. ..	

Registered letters must in all cases be handed in at the public counter half-an-hour before the box closes for ordinary correspondence.*

Telegraphs.

The only telegraph service at present in the Protectorate is that conducted by the African Trans-Continental Telegraph Company, whose line from Salisbury (South Rhodesia) and Tete (Portuguese territory) traverses the whole district between Chikwawa and Karonga, whence it is being carried to Lake Tanganyika and the Nile Valley.

The company has stations at Chikwawa (with a branch to Chiromo connecting with the Portuguese line), Blantyre, Zomba, Fort Johnston, Kota Kota, Florence Bay and Karonga. The station at Florence Bay is connected by telephone with a residential station at Kondowe, in the hills. The company has also a steamer on Lake Nyasa.

A Portuguese line connects Quelimane with Chiromo and Chindé, meeting the African Trans-Continental Telegraph system at the former place.

Telephone communication exists between Blantyre and Zomba and Liwondé. There is also a short line (2 miles) between the residency and the camp at Zomba.

* For further information as to postal services, see "British Central Africa Postal Guide," 1st January 1899.

CHAPTER VI.

ADMINISTRATION.

Districts. Civil Departments. Revenue. Currency.

Districts.   For administrative purposes, the Protectorate is divided into 12 districts, each possessing an administrative centre. These districts and centres are as follows :—

District.	Administration station.
Lower Shiré	Port Herald.
Ruo	Chiromo.
Mlanje	Fort Anderson.
Zomba	Zomba (Capital).
Blantyre	Blantyre.
West Shiré..	Chikwawa.
Upper Shiré	Liwondé.
South Nyasa	Fort Johnston.
Central Angoniland	Chiwere and Dedza.
Marimba	Kota Kota.
West Nyasa	Nkata.
North Nyasa	Karonga.

Zomba is the seat of the Government of the Protectorate, which is vested in a Commissioner, who is also Consul-General. Other Government officers are—

Deputy Commissioner and Consul ;
Assistant Deputy Commissioner and Vice-Consul ;
Vice-Consul at Chindé, who is also Agent and Post-master-General ;
Consular Agent and Postmaster at Chindé ;
Vice-Consul, Blantyre ;
Vice-Consul, Fort Johnston ;

and three grades of assistants.

Civil   The following departments are included in the administra-
Departments. tive services :—

1. Medical department consisting of a principal medical officer and staff of assistants, with establishments at Zomba, Blantyre, Fort Johnston, Chiromo, Mlanjé, and in Marimba; also 4 trained nurses, and hospitals for Europeans at Zomba and Blantyre.

2. Surveyors and public works department including—2 Europeon surveyors, 3 Indian surveyors; and a building and road staff of 3 Europeans—public works ; 2 Europeans—roads,

3. Scientific and forest department, with a European staff charged with the conservancy of Government forests, record of scientific observations, and conduct of experimental agriculture and planting.

Justice is administered to British subjects and other Europeans and foreigners under the Africa Orders in Council of 1891 and 1893, and to natives, as far as it is practicable, under native methods of procedure. *Judicial procedure.*

Special legislation relating to the internal government of the Protectorate is carried into effect by Regulations promulgated by the Commissioner after receiving the assent of the Secretary of State.

Civil police duties are carried out by a force of natives recruited locally, according to the requirements of each district. *Civil police.*

The Protectorate derives its revenue from Customs duties, tolls, rents of Crown lands, sale of timber, survey and judicial fees, stamp duties, licenses, and postal services, most of which are levied from settlers, and from a hut tax which is paid by natives, the present rate (1898) being 3s. per hut. *Revenue.*

English currency is used. *Currency.*

CHAPTER VII.

ARMED FORCES.

Military forces. Barracks. Fortified posts. Naval forces.

The military forces of the Protectorate include the troops allotted to Northern Rhodesia, and consist of a contingent of Sikhs and a native corps designated the British Central Africa Rifles.

Military forces. The Sikh contingent is composed of 215 men (of whom 40 are for service in Northern Rhodesia) lent by the Government of India for a period of 3 years, during which they are seconded in their regiments of the Indian Army.

Sikh contingent. The contingent furnishes the staff of the British Central Africa Rifles.

The European officers consist of—

1 Commandant,
1 Staff Officer,
1 Staff Officer for Northern Rhodesia,
1 Third Officer and Quartermaster,
1 Third Officer and Quartermaster for Northern Rhodesia.

These officers are seconded in the Indian Staff Corps for service in British Central Africa.

The Sikhs are distributed among the companies of the British Central Africa Rifles, so that each garrison of a fort is able to move out a complete force of Sikh and native troops to any point if called on to do so.

To the Sikh contingent are attached the usual camp followers as in India, also tailors and shoemakers.

British Central Africa Rifles. The British Central Africa Rifles were instituted in 1896, and are recruited entirely from the Atonga and Yao tribes.

The corps is enrolled under the British Central Africa Rifles Ordinance, 1897.

Establishment. Six companies, with a total establishment of seven British Officers, and 716 other ranks furnish the garrisons of the Protectorate.

Instructors. A Sikh colour-serjeant and three Sikh drill-instructors, drawn from the Indian Contingent are attached to each company.

Dress. The men wear a khaki uniform, with a black fez as full dress, and have also a blue undress uniform, with a red fez. The undress uniform, after the first issue, is kept up by the men themselves.

Equipment. Each man is provided with a blanket and haversack. The equipment used is the "Mackenzie" pattern, which admits of a blanket and 7 days' grain ration* being carried.

The rates of pay are—

Pay and rations.

Serjeants	..	..	..	10s. per mensem.
Corporals	..	..	..	7s. "
Privates	..	..	..	5s. "

with free rations, consisting of grain, rice and salt, or 2s. per mensem in lieu thereof.

The force has a battery of 2—9-pr. field guns, 4—7-pr. Guns. mountain guns and one Maxim. These guns are worked by native gun detachments under Sikh instructors.

A subordinate Medical Staff is a part of the military estab- Medical lishment. services.

The Protectorate force is at present armed with the Snider Arms. rifle, but these rifles are being replaced by the Martini-Enfield.

The distribution of the British Central Africa Rifles in the Distribution. Protectorate is as follows:—

Zomba (Head-quarters)	..	..	2 companies.
Mlanjé (Fort Lister)	..	..	1 company.
Mangoche	..	..	..	1 "
Kirk mountains (Fort Umlanjeni)	..	1 "
Marimba District	..	..	..	1 "
		Total	..	..	..	6

Two additional companies have been formed for garrisoning Northern Rhodesia, and a second battalion been raised for Imperial service in Mauritius.

In most of the stations brick buildings have been provided Barrack ac- for officers and wattle and daub huts for the Indian contingent. commodation. The men of the British Central Africa Rifles are accommodated in huts built by themselves.

Defensive posts in various parts of the Protectorate have Fortified been constructed in connection with operations against native posts. tribes, but in some cases where the object for which they were erected has been attained, they have not been kept up.

Fortified posts are, however, still necessary in certain districts where a garrison has to be maintained, either to check inroads or to prevent internal disturbances. They are established at the following places:—

Zomba.—Bastioned fort, built of brick, and loopholed. Used to guard stores, ammunition, arms, &c.

Mangoche.—Strong stone work, with ditch, occupied by garrison.

Fort Maguire.—A similar work, also containing accommodation for garrison, but not occupied at present.

Fort Alston.—Mwasi's, Marimba district. Strong earthwork, occupied by garrison.

---

* Mealies are the principal food of the natives who enlist in this corps. They are purchaseable at Blantyre at the rate of 2l. per ton.

Fort Manning.—Chirenje's, Central Angoniland. Stockade, earthwork and ditch. Contains accommodation for garrison.

Fort Umlanjeni, Kirk mountains.—Stockade and ditch. Occupied by garrison.

Fort Lister, Mlanjè.—Stockade, earthwork and ditch. Occupied by garrison.

Spare armament.

In addition to the armament noted above, there are in charge of the administration a certain number of Q.F. and machine guns, the property of the British South Africa Company.

Gunboats.

The Protectorate flotilla consists of four gunboats, the "Guendolen," "Adventure," "Pioneer" and "Dove," of which the first three are on Lake Nyasa, and the last-named on the Upper Shiré.

The "Adventure," "Pioneer" and "Dove" were sent out in sections from England under charge of Lieutenant Robertson, R.N. in 1893, and reconstructed by him on the lake. They remained under Admiralty supervision until the following year when they were taken over by the administration of the Protectorate.

The subjoined description shows their respective dimensions and armament.

"Guendolen."

1. "Guendolen."— Displacement, 350 tons; speed, 11 knots; complement, 50; steel twin-screw; draught, 5½ feet; fitted with electric searchlight; built by G. Rennie & Sons; launched on Nyasa, December 1898; not yet completed fitting. Armament, 4—3-pr. Hotchkiss Q.F. and 4—·303-inch Maxims.

"Adventure" and "Pioneer."

"Adventure" and "Pioneer."—Displacement, 35 tons; speed, 10 knots; complement, 17; steel screw; built by Yarrow & Sons; reconstructed on Nyasa, 1893. Armament, 1—7-pr. on boat-slide, two five-barrelled ·45-inch Nordenfelts, also field mountings for the same.

"Dove."

"Dove"— Displacement, 20 tons; speed, 7 knots; complement, 16; steel paddle steamer, light-draught river boat; built by Yarrow & Sons; reconstructed on Nyasa, 1893; armament, one five-barrelled ·45-inch Nordenfeldt, and field mounting for the same.

Other craft.

In addition to the gunboats, the Protectorate possesses on the Upper Shiré and Lake a barge, five steel boats and two sailing daus captured from Arab slave traders.

Service on the lake.
On Upper Shiré.

"The "Pioneer" and "Adventure" make regular monthly trips round the lake, and the "Dove," makes a weekly trip between Fort Johnston and Liwondé, and *vice-versâ*, carrying mail matter and Administration goods.

Naval head-quarters.

The naval head-quarters are at (New) Fort Johnston, where there are fitting and repairing yards, officers' quarters, &c.

The personnel consists of—

4 British Officers, Royal Naval Reserve,
3 European Engineers,
3 Indian Engineers,
3 British warrant officers (retired list, Royal Navy),

and about 40 trained negro seamen. Stokers are easily obtained from the lake coast tribes, and additional men for steamer and boatwork can always be depended on from the same source.

The Imperial Government provides for the defence of British interests on the Lower Shiré and Zambesi, Her Majesty's ships "Herald" and "Mosquito," river gunboats, being charged with that duty. Naval store depôts exist at Chindé and Chiromo.

CHAPTER VIII.

INDUSTRIES.

Trade. Exports. Imports. Coffee. Rubber. Other Products.
Domestic Animals.

Trade.

Trade in the Protectorate has steadily increased each year as the resources of the country developed. The returns for the year ending 31st March 1898 show a considerable increase in the totals both of imports and exports over the preceding 12 months, and though the number of European settlers has not been largely augmented during the last 2 years, the area of land under cultivation is larger and many Indian traders have come into the country and do a good business with the natives in small deals, which would hardly be worth the attention of the European merchants.*

Exports.

The chief articles of export are coffee, rubber and ivory; the two first show a steady increase during the last 4 years, while the quantity of ivory passing through the Protectorate has diminished greatly during the same period, large consignments from the west now finding their way to the coast through German and Portuguese territory. Other exports are hippopotamus teeth, beeswax, oil-seeds, and, latterly, the valuable drug strophanthus.

Imports.

Imports include alcohol, arms and ammunition, hardware, provisions and cotton goods, the last item being the largest. All these articles show an increase in 1897-98 over the preceding year.

Industries.
Coffee.

The principal industry occupying the attention of European settlers is the cultivation of the coffee plant, which owes its introduction into Nyasaland to Messrs. Duncan and Buchanan, of the Church of Scotland Mission, by whom the original plants were obtained from the Edinburgh Botanical Gardens in the

---

* The following notice with reference to the employment of Europeans in the Protectorate was published in the British Central Africa Gazette in December 1898:—" It is hereby made known that there is no employment to be had in this Protectorate for Europeans who come on the chance of obtaining work. A great deal of suffering and hardship has been experienced lately by Europeans who have come to Blantyre from Mashonaland, Natal, and South Africa generally, under the belief that employment and high wages could be easily obtained. This is not the case. The trading firms and others who employ Europeans have in every instance made arrangements for their staffs to be recruited from home; and, as persons are not appointed to places of trust without the fullest investigation into their antecedents, it is almost, if not quite, impossible to get work here from the trading companies and planters. Persons therefore who have not already secured an appointment in the Protectorate should not come here on the chance of obtaining employment, as this will only entail disappointment. Newspapers in Natal, Cape Colony, the Transvaal, and in Rhodesia are requested to copy."

year 1878. As the country became more settled and native labour available, plantations were formed on the plateaux of the Shiré Highlands, the chief centres being Blantyre, Zomba, Cholo and Mlanjé. Operations are now being extended to the West Nyasa and Central Angoniland districts.

The quality of the coffee grown is good and the quantity exported has risen from 40 tons in 1893 to 384 tons in 1898.

Rubber, next to coffee, the most important article of export, Rubber. is a natural product obtained from several species of indigenous plants. It is of good quality but the wasteful habits of the natives in its collection may result in a diminution of the trade, unless it is found that the rubber bearing plants can be successfully cultivated.

Tobacco is grown everywhere by the natives for the manu- Tobacco. facture of snuff. It has also been successfully cultivated by Europeans. Enough is now grown to supply the Protectorate, and endeavour is being made to cultivate it for export.

Tea planting has been tried, but is still in an experimental Tea. stage.

Rice is successfully cultivated at Kota Kota and other places, Rice. and is a valuable item in the food supply of the Indian and native population. It was originally introduced by the Arabs and Portuguese.

Wheat is grown is small quantities in the Shiré Highlands; Wheat. it is not used by the natives in this part of Central Africa.

Maize (Chimanga) and millet (Mapira or Mpemba) are the Other cereals. grain foods most used by natives; the millet is chiefly Maize. reserved for the manufacture of native beer. Maize is sold at Millet. Blantyre at the rate of 2l. per ton.

European potatoes have been introduced, and thrive well Vegetables. in certain localities. Among the vegetables found in the country are beans of several varieties, cassava or manioc, yams, and sweet potatoes, all much used by natives; also ground nuts, water melons, and pumpkins.

Sugar cane and plantains or bananas are grown for food, Sugar cane, and hemp for smoking. plaintains, hemp.

Oil for anointing and cooking purposes is obtained from the Oil. castor oil plant, the sesamum, and the oil palm.

Almost all the food plants have been introduced into Central Africa by Arabs and Portuguese.

Indigenous fruits are few in number, and have not been brought into cultivation. The lime and orange can be grown, and several fruits from temperate climates succeed in the higher districts.

Among the natives sowing operations usually commence with the early rains, and the harvest takes place in June and July.

Domestic animals found in the country include the ox, Domestic sheep, goat, dog, cat, fowl, muscovy duck, and pigeon. animals.

Horses, mules, and donkeys, where found, are a recent importation by European settlers. They do well in districts free from the tsetse fly.

Cattle.
The native cattle are mostly of the Zebu type, with a hump and short horns; a long horned breed with a straight back is, however, met with among the Angoni-Zulus on the plateaux south-west of Lake Nyasa, and is probably derived from a southern stock. The principal cattle-owning tribes are the Wankonde at the northern end of Nyasa, and the Angoni-Zulus in the south-west. The former are the only natives in British Central Africa who make use of cows' milk as an article of diet.

Sheep.
The sheep are of the fat-tailed breed, with hair instead of wool. The flesh is fairly good.

Goats.
Goats are extensively kept by all native tribes, and are valuable in many ways. The breed is a small one, with short horns and short hair.

Fowls.
Fowls are the staple flesh food of the European, and are plentiful and cheap.

Ducks.
The muscovy duck, introduced from Brazil by the Portuguese, is commonly found in the native villages.

CHAPTER IX.

MISSIONS.

The important share taken by missionaries in the earlier settlement of British Central Africa has already been noticed. Missionary work is still a very large factor in the civilization and education of the native races, and material progress in these respects has been made during the past few years. The following are the societies now possessing mission stations in the Protectorate :—

1. The Universities' Mission to Central Africa.—This, the Universities' first mission to Nyasaland, was founded in 1857, as the Mission. result of visits by Dr. Livingstone to Oxford and Cambridge. Its first establishment in Central Africa was formed near Zomba in 1859; the mission was constantly embroiled with the Yao tribes in that district, and after a struggle of over 3 years, withdrew in 1862 to Zanzibar, where it continued to work, and where its centre now remains. In 1881-82 the society again established a mission in Nyasaland, selecting as a station the island of Likoma, in Lake Nyasa, where interference by hostile tribes was less to be feared than on the mainland. Likoma, though by no means a healthy place, is still the head-quarters of the Mission in the Protectorate. There are also stations at Fort Johnston and Kota Kota, and several among the Yaos, on the east coast of Nyasa, with which communication is maintained by the mission steamer " Charles Janson." The staff consists of a bishop of Likoma and other clergy, a medical officer, ladies, and lay associates. In the numerous mission schools printing and other useful trades are taught by the lay associates. Most of the native Government printers at Zomba were thus trained.

2. The Livingstone Mission of the Free Church of Scotland.— Livingstone An expedition equipped by this society came out from Mission. Scotland in 1875 under Dr. Robert Laws, bringing with it the " Ilala," the first steamer placed on Lake Nyasa, and which is still running.

The original settlement of the mission was at Livingstonia, near Cape Maclear, but this site proving very unhealthy, its head-quarters were removed to Bandawe in West Nyasa, where much good work has been done among the Atonga and Angonis, as well as in connection with the study of native languages. Besides Bandawe, there are Free Church mission stations at Ekwendeni and Hora in West Nyasa; Kondowi, Ngerengi, and Karonga in North Nyasa, and at Mwengo on the Nyasa-Tanganyika plateau.

The mission has several qualified medical men among its members.

In its schools are taught carpentering and other trades and telegraphy.

Church of Scotland Mission.

3. Church of Scotland Mission.—This mission was founded at Blantyre in 1876. Its principal stations are at Blantyre and Zomba, and there are minor stations at Mlanjé, Chiradzulu and Pantumbi (Angoniland).

The staff comprises clergy, doctors, teachers and ladies. In the mission schools are taught elementary subjects in the vernacular and higher subjects in English; also carpentering, gardening, printing, building, cattle and dairy work, and for women and girls laundry work.

A mission steamer, the "Henry Henderson," plies on the Lower Shiré and Zambezi.

Dutch Reformed Church Mission.

4. The Dutch Reformed Church Mission.—This was originally established in 1889 as a branch of the Livingstone Free Church Mission. It has stations at Livelezi (South Nyasa District) and Mvera (Central Angoniland), besides schools at Kongwe, Livingstonia, Gowa, and other places in Angoniland. Industrial teaching is given in brickmaking, gardening, &c.

Zambesi Industrial Mission.

5. The Zambesi Industrial Mission was founded in 1892 by persons in England and Wales interested in the idea of the industrial development of Africa. Its religious teaching is undenominational, and it gives instruction in agriculture and various trades. It has stations at Mitsidi near Blantyre (headquarters), Chindé, Patuna (Lower Shiré), and at Lisungwi, Ndonda, Chiole and Dumbole (Upper Shiré).

Nyasa Baptist Mission.

6. The Nyasa Baptist Industrial Mission was started in 1892 and reorganized in 1894. Its head station is 4 miles north-west of Blantyre, and includes schools, shops, &c. The staff consists of four Europeans.

APPENDICES.

APPENDIX A.

NOTES ON THE BRITISH CONCESSIONS IN CHINDÉ.

Prior to the announcement in 1889 of Mr. D. Rankin's discovery of a navigable entrance to the Zambesi river by way of Chindé estuary, travellers and traders from the coast usually reached the Zambesi at Vicente by means of a boat journey up the Quaqua, followed by a land portage of 4 miles. This often took as much as 6 to 8 days in the dry season, whereas Vicente is now easily reached by river steamers from Chindé in less than 48 hours. *Former route to the Zambesi.*

The fact that vessels drawing as much as 20 feet of water can enter the port of Chindé and discharge cargo direct into river steamers and lighters, has led to a steady increase in its importance as a transit station for merchandize going to Central Africa.

In 1891, Mr. H. H. Johnston was instrumental in obtaining from the Portuguese Government, in consideration of an annual subsidy, the present British Concession, which is situated on the south bank of the Chindé estuary about 1 mile from its mouth. *Grant of British Concession.*

In return for this concession, a similar grant of land on the West Coast of Nyasa, at Point Kifu, was made to the Portuguese, but it has not, up to the present time, been occupied by them. *Portuguese Concession.*

By mutual agreement between the two Powers, the navigation of the Zambesi and its affluents was at the same time declared free to the merchant shipping of both nations.

The original British Concession had a frontage on the Chindé of ¼ mile, and a depth from the foreshore of 260 yards. Owing, however, to inroads of the river at the western end of the frontage, a considerable portion has been washed away, and, by a later agreement with the Portuguese, the depth has been increased at that point. *Chindé Concession.*

What is known as an "Outer Concession" extending southward to the sea, has been further granted for residential purposes, but does not carry with it the exemption from Portuguese customs duties, &c., which is conferred on the inhabitants of the British Concession proper whose numbers are limited to certain stated officials and representatives of trading concerns. *Outer Concession.*

The British Concession contains, besides Administration offices, bonded warehouses built on plots sublet to the various trading companies, who are thus enabled to store, free of duties, goods not intended for immediate transit.

The Postal Exchange Office for British Central Africa is situated in the concession, and is in charge of a resident Chief Postmaster, who is also Vice-Consul and Agent. Here mails are made up and exchanged with Europe and India, and with South and East Africa. *Postal establishment.*

Portuguese post office.	There is also a Portuguese post office at Chindé, which deals with mail matter for Portuguese territory only.
Ocean mails.	Ocean mails are conveyed to and from Chindé by a regular fortnightly service, calling at the time of new and full moon (spring tides) and owned by the following companies:—
Steamship lines.	Messrs. G. Rennie & Sons, trading between Durban and Quelimane and the Deutsche-Ost-Africa Line, running between Beira and Mozambique. Both lines call at intermediate ports.
Telegraph.	Chindé is connnected by telegraph with Quelimane, and thence with Chiromo and the African Trans-Continental system.
Harbour.	The Chindé Harbour is a good one, with plenty of water for a large number of vessels of deep draught.
Harbour Craft.	A hulk owned by a British firm is moored off the Concession, and several launches and lighters are available for harbour work.
Patent repairing slip.	There is also a patent slip for the repair of river steamers.
Health. Water.	Chindé is a healthy place, owing principally to its sea breezes. The water is not good; the drinking supply is obtained from rainwater
Domestic animals.	stored in iron tanks. Domestic animals, including horses, thrive; the tsetse fly is not found in the district.
Hotel. Stores.	There is an hotel with good accommodation, and European and Indian stores can be obtained.
Residences.	The majority of the residents live in the Outer Concession.

APPENDIX B.

NORTHERN RHODESIA.

Position and boundaries.	Under the term Northern Rhodesia* is included the whole of the region, except the strip forming the British Central Africa Protectorate, which lies between the Zambesi and the Congo Free State, and has as its eastern and western boundaries the Portuguese and German spheres.
	In 1891, the British South Africa Company were allowed by Her Majesty's Government, under certain conditions, to extend north of the Zambesi their field of operations under their charter of 1889; and it was arranged that Sir H. H. Johnston, Commissioner and Consul-General in Nyasaland, should undertake the administration of the northern portion in addition to his own duties, the Company paying a fixed annual contribution to the Protectorate police force, besides sharing other incidental expenses.
	This arrangement ceased in 1895, when the Company took the administration into their own hands.
Physical features. Mountains.	With the exception of the great valley of the Loangwa on the east, almost the whole of the country has an altitude of over 3,000 feet, and

---

* Barotseland, which forms the south-west portion of this region, has been described in a separate handbook compiled in the Intelligence Division in 1898.

at its northern end the Nyasa-Tanganyika plateau is in many places upwards of 6,000 feet above the sea level. The Mutshinga mountains west of the Loangwa also reach a considerable elevation.

The river system is very extensive, including as it does not only Rivers. great tributaries of the Zambesi such as the Loangwa and Kafue, but also the head waters of the Congo represented by the Chambesi and Luapula. These rivers do not appear to be navigable to any great extent even in the rains. The Zambesi for many hundred miles forms the southern boundary of the territory, and is navigable over certain portions in the wet season.

The only large lake lying wholly within the British sphere is Lakes. Bangweolo, fed by the Chambesi, and drained by the Luapula. Its area has been estimated by Livingstone and others at upwards of 1,600 square miles, but it varies greatly, according to the season of the year.

Lake Tanganyika, the largest lake but one in Africa, forms part of the northern limit of British Central Africa; it is over 400 miles in length, and from 30 to 60 wide, and is navigable everywhere. It does not receive any important affluents from the south.

Lake Mweru, through which the Luapula flows on its way north-ward, is also part of the northern boundary. It is about 68 miles long by 24 wide, and navigable throughout the year.

Between Tanganyika and Mweru lies an extensive salt marsh, also called Mweru, which is flooded in the wet season.

A small lake named Lake Moir is situated in the mountain range west of the central portion of the Luangwa valley.

The European inhabitants are at present confined to officials, Inhabitants. missionaries and a few settlers.   Europeans.

The natives are of the same Bantu-Negro stock as those in the Natives. Protectorate, but represent different groups for the most part. The most important tribes are those of the Awemba group, living in the northern part, and the Barotse and Wasenga in the centre and south. Formerly there were many Arab settlements scattered about the country, but with the suppression of the slave trade, which formed their occupation, their numbers have greatly decreased. The Awemba are said to be a fine race physically, and to be opposed to European intervention.

The general conditions of climate, temperature, and health are Climate and similar to those existing in the British Central Africa Protectorate. health.

The present avenues of approach to Northern Rhodesia are by way Communica-of the Shiré and Lake Nyasa, either from Liwondé or Kota Kota to the tions. Loangwa or from Karonga by the Stevenson road to Lake Tanganyika. The latter route, 140 miles from the Protectorate boundary, has been made available for wagon transport.

Postal communication is conducted through the Protectorate Postal service. service, viâ Kota Kota or Karonga.

The African Trans-Continental Telegraph Company is extending its Telegraphs. operations from Karonga through the northern part of the country.

The first steps towards internal government were made by Sir H. H. Administra-Johnston, who divided the north of the territory into four districts, to tion. which another in the south-east has since been added.

These districts are named Chambesi, Tanganyika, Mweru, Luapula, and Luangwa, and are administered by collectors in principal stations, and assistant collectors in sub-stations.

The stations and sub-stations are as follows :—

District.	Principal station.	Sub-station.
Chambesi	Ikawa	Nyala.
Tanganyika..	Aberoorn .. .. {	Mambwe. Sambu (police station).
Mweru	Rhodesia	Choma.
Luapula	.. ..	.. ..
Loangwa	Fort Jameson	.. ..

The head-quarters of the Administration are temporarily at Aber-corn.*

Police.   A force of civil police composed of 80 Makua (coastmen), and about 230 natives is distributed among the different stations and sub-stations under the orders of the Administration officers.

Military force.   The military garrison of the country is included in the forces under the orders of the Commandant, British Central Africa Protectorate, and consists at present of 40 Sikhs, and about 250 native troops of the British Central Africa Rifles.

Arms.   The armament (machine guns, rifles, &c.), belonging to the company is also under the control of the Protectorate Government.

Trading stations.   Trading stations belonging to the African Lakes Company are established at Fife, on the Stevenson Road (Chambezi district), and on Lake Tanganyika, and the Rhodesia Concessions Company has a station near Fort Jameson, Loangwa district.

Missions.   The Free Church Mission, and a French mission (Péres Blancs) have stations on the northern plateau and Lake Tanganyika.

APPENDIX C.

GERMAN EAST AFRICA.

Geographical position.   The German sphere of influence in East Africa, a portion of which forms the northern boundary of British Central Africa, extends west-ward from the Zanzibar coast to Lake Tanganyika, and northward from the Ruvuma river and Lake Nyasa to British East Africa and Victoria Nyanza, thus having access within its limits to all three of the great African lakes.

Administration.   The Administration of German East Africa is carried out under direct Imperial control through resident European officers at 8 stations on the coast and 11 inland.

The head-quarters of the Administration are at Dar-es-Salaam on the coast.

The Administration centre for Lake Nyasa and the district border-ing on British Central Africa is at Langenburg at the north-east end of the lake. The station for Lake Tanganyika is Ujiji on the eastern shore.

European population.   The number of Europeans in German East Africa in 1898 is returned as being 880, of whom 665, including officials, are Germans. Of other Europeans, the greater part are French, English, Dutch, and Swiss missionaries, and the remainder chiefly Levantine traders, &c.

---

* Arrangements for the future administration of Northern Rhodesia are now under consideration.

The armed forces consist of 122 Europeans, 1,634 Protectorate Armed forces. troops, and 444 police, with 43 guns.

The Protectorate troops (Schutztruppen) are composed of 12 companies, varying in strength from 48 to 176, of mixed Sudanese and natives, and 152 special service troops, similarly made up, the numbers being respectively, Sudanese, 466, and natives, 1,168.

The police (Polizeitruppen) consist of 296 Sudanese and 148 natives.

These troops and police are distributed among the various stations in accordance with local requirements, most of the posts being provided with one or more guns.

The force in the Langenburg district numbers 2 Europeans, 20 Sudanese, and 32 natives, with 2 guns; that at Ujiji consists of 8 Europeans, 53 Sudanese and 97 natives, with 3 guns.

The native troops are chiefly drawn from the following tribes:— Nyamwesi, Nyema, Swahili and Sukuma.

The period of service is 2½ years, with a re-engagement for a similar period. Period of service.

A Government steamer, the "Hermann von Wissmann," is placed Government on Lake Nyasa, and makes monthly trips between Langenburg and vessels. Fort Johnston. This vessel was brought out in 1892 by Major von Wissmann, who was in command of an expedition, equipped at the instance of the German Anti-Slavery Society, to assist in the suppression of the slave trade on Lake Nyasa.

A steamer destined for Lake Tanganyika was sent out to Chindé early in 1898, to be conveyed overland.

The great northern caravan road followed by the Arab slave traders Communica-coming from Central Africa passed through what is now German tions. territory, on the way to the Zanzibar coast from the head of Lake Caravan road. Nyasa, but since the suppression of the traders, the route has fallen into disuse.

A postal route exists between the stations on Lake Nyasa and Postal route. Kilwa on the sea coast.

A railway, 25 miles long. connects Tanga with Muhesa, and was Railway. opened for traffic early in 1896. It has been taken over by the Government this year, and is to be extended as far as Korogwe, about 50 miles from Tanga.

Surveys have been made for a railway from Dar-es-Salaam to Ujiji on Lake Tanganyika, but so far no steps have been taken to raise money for its construction.

Langenburg is situated on a somewhat unhealthy peninsula, and Langenburg. has an indifferent anchorage. The European population of the district numbers 55, chiefly missionaries, one society of whom is established at Mlaudala (Berlin Mission).

APPENDIX D.

PORTUGUESE EAST AFRICA.

Portuguese East Africa comprises the provinces of Mozambique Geographical and Lorenço Marques, the former being to the north and the latter to position. the south of the Zambesi.

D

Administration. The administration is carried out by a Royal Commissioner, who is appointed for 3 years, and resides in the capitals of the respective provinces alternately. Each settlement on the coast has its own municipality and the usual machinery of administration.

Mozambique Company. The Mozambique Company, which has a Royal Charter granting sovereign rights for 25 years from 1891, administers the districts of Manica and Sofala.

Armed forces. The Portuguese forces in East Africa, according to the latest available information, are as follows:—

European troops—
1 battery Artillery
2 squadrons Cavalry. } Total, 683.
2 companies Infantry.

Colonial troops—
1 company, Mozambique Engineers.
1 battery, Lorenço Marques Artillery.
Section Mozambique Artillery.
Section Zambesi Artillery.
Section Inhambane Artillery.
Section Gaza Artillery.
1 squadron, Dragoons of Lorenço Marques.
1 squadron, Dragoons of Gaza.
9 companies, Rifles.
1 disciplinary battalion.
5 depôts.
1 veteran company.

The estimated total of the above is about 2,500. They are mostly officered by Goanese.

The garrisons north of the Zambesi in 1890 were—

At Mozambique—about 2,000.
At Sena—30 regulars, 500 irregulars.
At Zumbo—30 regulars, 500 irregulars.
At Tete—30 regulars, 60 irregulars.
At Ibo Island—about 30 men.

There is a Portuguese post at Chiromo opposite the British settlement.

Gunboats. Several small gunboats or launches armed with small bore revolving cannon and machine guns are placed on the Zambesi and adjacent waters. They are borne on the strength of the Portuguese Navy.

Chindé. There is a Portuguese customs station at Chindé, and a dock and slip for the river gunboats is said to have been constructed some years ago.

Native tribes.* In the territory north of the Zambesi the native population is composed partly of indigenous races, and partly of tribes who have invaded the coast country from the westward, and have formed settlements.

To the former class belong the Makua, living between the sea coast and the River Lujenda; the Yao on the Lujenda and in the mountainous district east of Lake Nyasa, and the Manganja on the Upper Lujenda.

The invading races are of Zulu origin, and are distributed in the region between Lake Nyasa and the coast.

* Nyasa Portuguez, por V. Almeida d'Eça Nevista, Portugueza Coloniale Maritima, December 1898.

APPENDIX E.

OUTFIT FOR OFFICERS OF THE ARMED FORCES, BRITISH CENTRAL AFRICA.

The following suggestions as to the outfit required, are offered for the use of officers newly appointed to British Central Africa.

It is better to bring the articles required from England, as although camp equipment, guns, furniture, &c., may be occasionally obtained from officers leaving the country, the supply from this source cannot be depended on, and the necessary articles cannot be purchased locally.

The officers of the armed forces are stationed in forts about the country, often by themselves, and only those of Indian Staff Corps and Royal Artillery can depend upon remaining at head-quarters, Zomba. It should be remembered that the climate at most of the military posts is frequently cold, and warm clothes, blankets, &c., are essential.

Uniform.—The uniform worn is khaki drill, putties and shooting boots, khaki helmet of Egyptian or Indian pattern, and Sam Browne belt, with the usual articles of an officer's equipment.

The khaki drill can be obtained and made up in Zomba. Cloth uniform is not required, with the exception of mess-dress for official dinners, &c., nor are white uniform, jack boots, or spurs.

Plain clothes.—At least one warm suit of tweed or serge, with several of flannel, which is most constantly worn. For shooting, gabardine, being rain and thorn proof, is recommended. Shirts for ordinary wear and with uniform should be of flannel or some similar material, as also sleeping suit. Evening dress and a few white shirts, &c. Riding breeches and gaiters.

Hats.—For ordinary wear, a "shikar," or double terai hat, straw hat and cap. For shooting, a brown "shikar," or, if obtainable, a pith sun hat ("solar topi"), which is much the best.

Boots.—These should be stout shooting boots, as the wear is excessive, and several pairs should be brought out, as also of tennis shoes. A pair of indiarubber knee boots is invaluable.

Waterproofs.—These should have sewn and gummed seams, and should be strong, to resist the heavy rainfall.

Camp equipment.—The following are absolute necessaries :—

Tent.—The best pattern is the Indian-Cabul tent of 120 lbs., or the double fly (No. 2 Wissmann size) tent of green rot-proof canvas.

Camp bed of wood, not iron. but stout enough to stand knocking about.

Folding washstand, with iron basin, table, chair.

Small camp lantern and a Lord's patent lantern in iron case.

Canteen fitted with kettle, pots, plates, dishes, &c., of not too small a size.

Bath.—The most useful form is the ordinary travelling bath, with lid, lock, and strap, fitted with a basket inside, in which one's whole kit can be carried.

Waterproof ground sheet.
Wolseley valise.
Wire pillow.
Mosquito curtains.
Table-cloths and napkins.

Guns.—A ·303 Lee-Metford sporting rifle and a shot gun are all that are required for general shooting, with a plentiful supply of cartridges.

Jeffery's bullets for the rifle. For the gun the best shot are No. 4 and a few No. 8, and gun cartridges should be loaded with black powder.

There is excellent fishing of all kinds to be obtained on the rivers and lakes.

Saddlery is not required, as there are few horses in the country.

Bicycles.—If a machine is brought out, it should be fitted with "tropical" tyres, and spare inner tubes should be brought.

Stores and provisions can be obtained locally, but it is better to bring out a supply of wine, &c., with some champagne for use in case of sickness.

Newspapers.—Arrangements should be made for a supply of newspapers and periodicals, which should be addressed to Zomba.

Amongst sundries, the following will be found most useful :— Cavalry sketching case, aneroid, compass, small medicine chest, clinical thermometer, and a hair clipping machine.

Officers should bring out a last-pay certificate, as without it they cannot draw their pay in British Central Africa.

APPENDIX F.

Works of Reference.

i. Official Publications.

Report on First 3 Years' Administration of British Central Africa. C. 7504, 1894.

Report on Trade and General Condition, British Central Africa Protectorate, 1895-96. C. 8254, 1896.

Report on Trade and General Condition, British Central Africa Protectorate, 1896-97. C. 8438, 1897.

Annual Report, British Central Africa Protectorate, 1897-98. C. 9048, 1898.

Report of Trade of British Central Africa, 1894. C. 7581-55, 1895.

Reports of Operations against Slave Traders in British Central Africa. C. 7925, 1896.

Statistical Abstract, Colonial Possessions. C. 8993, 1898.

ii. General Publications.

British Central Africa, by Sir H. H. Johnston, K.C.B., 1897.

Adventures in Nyasaland, by L. Monteith-Fotheringham, 1891.

Explorations in the Country West of Lake Nyasa. Journal, Royal Geological Society, August 1897.

Das Deutsch Afrikauische Schutzgebiet, by Carl Peters, 1895.

Deutsch Ostafrika, by F. Wohltmann, 1898.

As Colonias Portuguezas, by E. J. de C. e Vasconcellos, 1897.

British South Africa Company Report, 1896-97.

Africa. Vol. ii. South Africa, by A. H. Keane, 1895.

iii. Languages.

Swahili.

Handbook of the Swahili Language, by Bishop Steere, revised and enlarged by A. C. Madan.

English-Swahili Dictionary, compiled for the use of the Universities Mission, British Central Africa.

Yao.

Second Yao-English Primer, by R. S. Hynde.

Yao-English Vocabulary, by W. Maples.

Collections for a handbook of the Yao language, by Bishop Steere.

Chinyanja.

Vocabulary, Society for Promoting Christian Knowledge.

Henry's Grammar, published by Fraser, Aberdeen.

Exercise Book (Woodward), Society for Promoting Christian Knowledge.